A Necklace of Bees

A Necklace of Bees

POEMS BY

Dannye Romine Powell

The University of Arkansas Press
Fayetteville
2008

Copyright © 2008 by The University of Arkansas Press

ISBN-10: 1-55728-879-8
ISBN-13: 978-1-55728-879-0

12 11 10 09 08   5 4 3 2 1

Text design by Ellen Beeler

⊖ The paper used in this publication meets the minimum requirements
of the American National Standard for Permanence of Paper
for Printed Library Materials Z39.48-1984.

Library of Congress Cataloging-in-Publication Data

Powell, Dannye Romine.
A necklace of bees : poems / by Dannye Romine Powell.
p. cm.
ISBN-13: 978-1-55728-879-0 (pbk. : alk. paper)
ISBN-10: 1-55728-879-8 (pbk. : alk. paper)
I. Title.
PS3566.O8267N43 2008
811'.54—dc22
2008015312

For Lew, always,
for Hugh & Alyssa,
for Ashley & Taylor

Acknowledgments

Grateful acknowledgment is made to the editors of the following publications in which these poems originally appeared, some in slightly different versions: *Atlanta Review:* "The Train Whistle"; *Bellevue Literary Review:* "It Is Said That Wigmakers"; *Beloit:* "Loss Considers the Idea of Bliss"; "Loss Received a Letter Once"; *Charlotte Writers' Club Anthology:* "Why I Miss Visiting My Mother-in-Law in Helena, Arkansas"; *Comstock Review:* "Two Sisters in Their Gabardine Skirts"; *Kakalak:* "The Villa"; *Nimrod:* "You Have Ruined Us for the Pragmatic World"; "Dying from the Feet Up"; "The Stepping-Stone Kit"; *Paperstreet:* "Briefly, I Was Asleep"; *Ploughshares:* "The Avalanche"; *Tar River Poetry Review:* "This Morning"; "Everyone Is Afraid of Something"; *Two Rivers:* the second stanza of the poem now entitled, "Your Beautiful Hands."

The poems, "You Have Ruined Us for the Pragmatic World," "Dying from the Feet Up," and "The Stepping-Stone Kit," were finalists in the 2005 Pablo Neruda Poetry Prize Contest sponsored by *Nimrod.*

The poem, "The Train Whistle," was a finalist in the 2007 *Atlanta Review* International Poetry Contest.

The author would like to express grateful appreciation to the Foundation of Yaddo for a three-week residency in the winter of 2004 in Sylvia Plath's former bedroom. The poem "This Morning" was written while gazing out the window of Ted Hughes's former study in West House.

Contents

I
Everyone Is Afraid of Something

II
The Earth Beneath the Earth

III
The Dual Nature of Grief

A Necklace of Bees

I

Everyone Is Afraid of Something

Loss Waits on the Porch

I rented a farm house once at the foot of a mountain.
Each morning, cows drifted close
to the door and stared without seeing.
This was before cell phones,
and my mother-in-law was nervous
I'd gone off for a week
to a place where no one could reach me.
A pale dirt road wound through close trees,
no other houses in sight.
Maybe she thought I was meeting a lover,
though I don't remember that my husband worried.
When I arrived, I plugged in my typewriter,
set water on to boil. Then I let you in
the side door. I'd heard you out there,
your ferny breath.

The Child and I

i.

Cross-legged in spring grass,
a platter of sliced apples
between us, we tossed the crescents
high into twilight. A silly game
to pass the evening. Her slices,
I began to notice, held fast
in the expanse of sky, exploded
into stars, while mine fell back
time and again to earth. How easy
she made it look, arms supple
and tan against her ivory
dress, honeyed hair swinging
to her waist. I watched, enchanted,
wondering if I'd merely forgotten
how to tantalize the air—or if I ever knew.

ii.

I will call the feeling grace.
I stared at the baby
in my lap, an ill-conceived notion
already swiping at my heart. *This can't be
my son's,* I said to the long-haired girl
on the couch. Rude. I knew better,
and knew it was his—his olive skin,
my mother's deep dimples
trespassing time. I sat there,
in the girl's brown chair,

the stunned feeling pulsing
through me
like sea water. Something
like love in its wake.

iii.

I dream
the pyracantha back,
its bulge and tangle lush
once more along the far brick wall,
leaves glossy, its muscled trunk
lean and pale.

And there again
on the lawn
that wondrous child, the one
we were fools enough
to believe would save us all,
gown rumpled, face flushed,
one finger out for me
to pluck the thorn, a seed
of blood forming like a berry.

Everyone Is Afraid of Something

Once I was afraid of ghosts, of the dark,
of climbing down from the highest
limb of the backyard oak. Now I'm afraid

my son will die alone in his apartment.
I'm afraid when I break down the door,
I'll find him among the empties—bloated,
discolored, his face a stranger's face.

My granddaughter is afraid of blood
and spider webs and of messing up.
Also bees. Especially bees. Everyone,
she says, is afraid of something.

Another fear of mine: that it will fall to me
to tell this child her father is dead.

Perhaps I should begin today stringing
her a necklace of bees. When they sting
and welts quilt her face, when her lips
whiten and swell, I'll take her
by the shoulders. *Child, listen to me.*
One day, you'll see. These stings
are nothing. Nothing at all.

I Stopped Drinking in Hopes Loss Would Stop, Too

Bought a long, velour robe,
all rosy folds and sober
pockets. That first night I brushed
my teeth twice, sat propped
in my white-tiled thoughts
scrubbed of grime and mildew.
Loss didn't last the day,
said he could feel bristles
sprouting in his head, said the soles
of his feet itched. He knew
exactly what would fix it, of course.
So Loss carries on still, tapping
on my window, palms to the stars.
Let me back in, he whines. I crack
the door, high on one whiff of him.

Daddy Tosses Them Down

then tosses Baby
in the air. Sometimes he tickles her
or snaps at her legs with his tie.
Other times, he begs Baby to recite
the rhyme about the kitty. She'll say it
any time because she likes to hear him laugh:

I love little pussy,
her coat is so warm . . .

Again, he says. *Do it again.*

I love little pussy,
her coat is so warm . . .

Keep going, he says.

And if I don't hurt her,
she'll do me no harm.

Daddy rocks back and forth,
roaring, *More! More!*

Mommy cries,
Stop! Mommy wears pearls
and tries to keep things smooth
and in order. Forks
with forks. Spoons with spoons.

Mommy tells Baby to go play
with her toys. Which she does,
tossing her blonde doll high
in the air, and higher still,
hoping she won't
hurt her, hoping she will.

Loss Received a Letter Once

scrawled, on ruled paper, from a woman
who knew his parents in their youth,
her words a lit path through thickets of old
confusions. He'd open it and the photo
always fell out—him and his silly-proud grin,
lofting a toy boat, his mother in khaki
shorts and knit shirt. He'd hold
a magnifying glass to study her hand
and how it lingered on his shoulder. He lost
the letter, of course—maybe it landed in the trash
by mistake, maybe he stashed it in a book. He looks
for it still, its choppy, blue lake of regret,
the little boat bobbling to a distant shore.

The Avalanche

He braked
the old green Chevy
on the side
of a mountain
somewhere out West
and bet my mother
he could start an avalanche
by kicking
a single rock
into another. *No,*
she said, *no, please*
don't, Dan, please.

And in the back
seat, I, an only child,
trapped with a pile
of Archie and Veronicas,
watched my mother's chin
crumple
while out the window
my father hunted
the sun-crazed slope
for that one rock
that would knock
our whole world loose.

You Have Ruined Us for the Pragmatic World

There was a time, Eliacim, when you and I liked Viennese waltzes...,
which are best listened to dressed as a tree...

        —*Mrs. Caldwell Speaks to Her Son,* a novel by Camilo José Cela

I am onto you, Mrs. Caldwell,
as I was onto my own mother,
who could spend hours dressed as a tree,
her favorite the weeping willow. The pity
is how, from birth, you pull us in,
ruining us for the pragmatic world.

You write to Eliacim
that Viennese waltzes are not favorable
for love, that they are suited
for the monotonous arts
of marriage. Love, you proclaim, is *arhythmical.*
Such pretense, Mrs. C. Why did you not teach him

to endure the niggling rigors of daily life?
Don't answer. We know. You ask Eliacim
to remember when Viennese waltzes
made the two of you very happy, those waltzes,
you tell him, to which one must dance
barefoot or in golden slippers.

Certain words, Mrs. C., we mothers must not utter
to our sons. I keep a list. *Slippers* is one. *Lilac*
another. *Wreath. Tremble. Perfumed. Silk.*
Flutter. And, *barefoot,* of course.

Two Sisters in Their Gabardine Skirts

and form-fitting sweaters
and their mother, the color of chalk,
in the walnut bed, dying.
What is there to do? The sisters
don't know, and the old woman can't
even speak. Out the windows,
the March wind troubles
the tops of the ancient
trees. Nothing stirs
the sisters. Their turbulence
blows underground, afternoon
and night, careening
into the hollows. You wish
they'd wring their hands,
those identical fingers
that can span more
than an octave. Or try
to pick out the tune
of their love. A sip
of water, perhaps. A cool
cloth. Or simply fling open
their arms and jitterbug
out of their skin.

My Mother's Lips

The frenzy of them
that Sunday after church
when she beckoned me over
to meet her friends, a couple, new members
maybe, and snaked out a long arm
to draw me near—I was fifteen or sixteen—
and it was warm, a sweet Miami day,
palm trees, red hibiscus, the ocean
a breeze away, my boyfriend's house
a fast mile down the street, and those lips
quivered as if she were freezing, quivered
as if she were fevered, quivered as if to say, *Don't
dare embarrass me!* and I wasn't sure how
but I knew any second I'd go wrong
and even now that she's dead, I fear I might
write something in this line or the next, something—
I never know what—that could still sink us both.

How Her Words Entered Me When She Called to Say My Father Had Died at Last after Ten Months of Pain

entered me the way we entered the coral rock caves
at the edge of Venetian Pool, if we could muster the nerve
to brave the caves at all and, because we were girls,
did so only on a dare from some cowlicked
fifth- or sixth-grade boy because we had to duck
under and make our way blind through the black,
watery depths until we reached a ledge
at the back of the caves where we sat panting
while the fear drained off, and now, chattering,
another breath, one more plunge, and we crashed
to the far opening until, still swimming, we burst
into light, lifting our wet faces to an anthem
of blue and green—released into Eden.

After the Stroke

My mother propped
in my wide bed,
her new mind layered
and more mysterious
than ever.

She wept for weeks,
clinging to me,
pleading to return home,
to drive again, promising
to stay off the freeways.
A new word for her—freeways—
as if the assault
on her brain had taught her
the nature of danger.

I'd watch her watching me
at the mirror,
as if she were trying
to remember something
she'd lost. Finally, I believed
she loved me.

Tending her,
I often felt I'd swallowed stones,
the way long ago
she'd swallowed me
whole, then flown off
to land all these decades later
in my midst, crippled, free.

Loss Touched Death Once

The hair was there. Eyebrows, cheeks.
Small, disheveled mouth. He'd seen this arrangement
before. Somewhere. Maybe. Wanted to pinch it.
Wanted to slap sweet sense into it.

II

The Earth Beneath
the Earth

All I Know for Certain

After the phone call,
we drove morning and night,
knocked and knocked on the hard, loved door.
You answered in your soft brown voice, your skirt drifting
into drowsy folds. In the fire-lit room where your mother lay
cold, arms folded, I studied your face for traces
of sorrow, studied the bed. I couldn't imagine how
you had stayed so calm until the morning you died and I folded
your arms.

It Is Said That Wigmakers

simply by the sense of smell
can tell whether the hair
is from combings or has been cut

from the living. What about this
tendril I clipped from your head
moments after you died

because I could not leave
all of you there on the table
under the strange light.

The Gaudy Clothes of Tourists

In the mornings, without anyone's seeing me, I would disinter you care-
fully, my love, so you could breathe.

—Mrs. Caldwell

Please, Mrs. C., you're not the first
to want to disinter. Emerson unearthed two
coffins. Months after Ellen died, he pried the lid
to look once more on his sweet wife.
Then his little Waldo, dead at five of scarlet fever.
He waited fifteen years to gaze again
upon that child's face.

You do not suffer alone, Mrs. C.,
though that's not my point exactly. For you,
the act is settled. Your Eliacim died
with his shipmates at sea. Gone.
Irretrievable. My son's death
is incomplete, only a fear, though
as his drinking increases, a fear that daily grows.

See how I'm learning from you,
Mrs. Caldwell. How I weave my sad skein
into something gaudy, like the clothes
the tourists wore on winter days in Miami.
Too bright, too skimpy, their arms broiled red
in the sun. But we who lived there year-round,
we who were young and sedate in our dark cotton
dresses, we who had not yet borne sons,
we could not tear our eyes away.

23

This Morning

More snow and the phone call
I've been dreading. Not the one that says
he's dead. The one that says he's drinking again.
Nothing I can do here, in these deep woods,
a thousand miles from home. The green branches
can hold the white so long, then it flies, scattering.
Icicles that hung for days like pipe organs
at my window, gone now, and with them
the imagined chords. All morning, snow
thuds down on itself, numbing whatever tries to breathe.

Loss Dreams He Hears Sobbing

when he answers the phone, sobbing without ceasing,
without surfeit, sobs lodged in the throat, sobs
coming loose, sobs on their knees begging
forgiveness. Sobs like that. Loss tosses all night.

Dying from the Feet Up

Yesterday I was ill, my dear, when I was writing you; I didn't have the
strength to reach the bedroom . . .

—Mrs. Caldwell

Mrs. C., may I introduce Mary Todd Lincoln,
whose grief surely equals your own. Little Eddie
dead at three, tender Willie at eleven, and, at twenty,

her dark-eyed, faithful Tad. Such martyrs, the two
of you—from London, Mary writes to son Robert:
I scarcely imagined when I began this letter

that my strength would hold out for more
than three pages. Mrs. C., do you agree
these complaints are nothing more than manipulation,

intended to fish your sons from their icy depths?
I'll speak plain: One evening, when I was ten,
I sat making potholders, content

until my mother announced she was dying
from the feet up. Imagine! Mrs. C., I tell you, I stared
at her legs, slim, white stalks pressed together

and began working my hook in and out
of those bright strands as if nothing mattered
but my weaving. I've wondered since if, like you,

she, too, wanted to pluck from me
something I could not yet give. I felt a traitor,
sitting there, feigning indifference. I'll admit to you

I've been tempted to try this ploy with my own son.
But recalling that evening and my dogged silence,
I must say I consider the tactic nothing but unwise.

Loss Calls the Cops

He's done this before.
Calls the cops
to say his best friend
went fishing and won't answer
his phone. Loss stands on the bank,
brow furrowed, watching the divers
and inhaling the smell
of the muck the wrecker pulls up.
There's never anybody there.
It's just that feeling he gets
sometimes, that bloated feeling,
chains dragging his chest.

When He Told Her

and she knew from the beginning
he must
one day tell her,
she thought of that banyan tree—he would remember
the one—and how over the long years
it had fastened itself to the earth and the earth beneath
the earth, its long roots once suspended
in air now anchoring an orphanage of limbs, the leaves
beneath the leaves marshaling the dark, as if to say, *Come,*
I will hold you, you and your tears, so dense
was its shade, so bold the branches, so ferociously attached.

Why She Plants Lavender

Because
she depends
on one kind
to range
on its belly
like purple fog,
its hush lingering.

On another
to fatten
into globes
of silvery breath,
whispery, strong,
like sunlit avenues
of song.

On yet another,
because no matter
how drenched
in perfume, this one
refuses to wilt
late afternoons,
its tender spikes
holding sorrow
upright, dignified.

Your Beautiful Hands

i.

For years,
I've watched your hands,
your beautiful hands,
the way they moved
like reasonable arguments,
their princely hesitations
always insisting
that everything was
as it seemed,
that the moon wouldn't spill
its pocked truth
into our mouths,
that the contours
of love would conform
to our lies.

ii.

In the first dark
of evening
the man's song
across the back alley
dreamed through us
like a river of stars.

Mornings,
scrubbed patches
of light at our feet,
we imagined

where he'd sat—there,
on the low bench
under the oak,
his back to the trunk,
that cleansing voice
melted into night.

iii.

After I stopped dreaming
about you, the rooms continued
in color, night
after night, all that
familiar space empty
of you. I open a door,
hoping to find you,
hoping to dance
you back
into the narrows
of the dream. Nothing.

I struggle
to enter the dream
that precedes
these dreams, the one
where August presses flat
as a handkerchief
against the panes,
where you are
locating our place
in the book and I am curled
close, hands folded,
surprised, always,
by what happens next.

She Told Me the Dead Woman's Husband Had Been Running Around for Years

I was folding small blue shirts
when she told me, stacking them
on a shelf. The dead woman
was my friend. I had just come
from her funeral.
Stack. Stack. Stack.
I made rows, without counting,
which was unlike me. Neither
did I hold a single one
to my cheek, as I might have done earlier.
There were also larger shirts. I folded
those, too. I was very neat, much neater
than in real life.
I kept on folding and stacking.
I saw no end to it. Still, I did not tire.
I do remember not being able
to anticipate how high each stack
would rise
without collapse.

The Train Whistle

At dawn, I wait
for the whistle.
I can almost see the waking
passengers, yawning,
clothes askew,
how they stare out
into the thickets
of pine, their minds
trying to embrace the blunder
and hum of their lives.

Only when
the whistle blows
do they face what is true—
that our lives are lived
and unlived, that the past
and future are pooling
into one as the train breaks
into morning,
closer and closer.

To say I wait
for the whistle
is not entirely true.
It's as if the whistle
waits for me.
Or, forgive my conceit,
longs for me.
As if during the night,

the engines have gathered speed,
churning black air
into hot, urgent waves.

When I hear the oval scream
I throw open my windows.
Day after day, I lean out
into rain, into sun,
into snow, arms wide
and amazed,
the whistle wailing
and wailing,
all that is lost, all that is not.

Arranging a Life

A woman digs up her prize
coreopsis, covers the disgruntled ground
with cedar chips. Soon she's tossing old love
letters, hand-stitched baby clothes.
It's as if she's been bitten
by an urge to clean out, rename

what she keeps. She calls the lamp
by her bed a moon. The bed, she says,
is a bay she swam as a child, blue
beyond belief, her breath ragged as she pulls
toward shore, a shore she calls by a name
she swore she'd never breathe again.

Poem Beginning with a Line from Walker Percy

Have you noticed
that the narrower the view
the more you can see?
What about the son
who, time after time, slumps
against the night, lost.
When I peer into the well
of his being, I find moss,
old stone, the cool dank
of indifference. Finally,
my own face in the round
of glassy water. Nothing
more, though I keep staring
into the dark, trying
to believe in unseen springs
routing through earth,
bubbling up with an abundance
to slake the sorriest thirst.

Loss Says He's Moving to the Beach

Says the salt air will clear
his sinuses, allow him to cough up
the phlegm that's troubled him

all winter. I hope he goes now,
while morning drubs cold light
through me. By late afternoon,

I might stumble onto something
he forgot: one brown sock,
a half-empty pack of Marlboros,

his old Hohner Big River harmonica.

Events

There are very important people, Eliacim, . . . who are excessively fond
of events, accidents, derailments, rapes and murders.

—Mrs. Caldwell

That fondness makes sense to me, Mrs. C.
I've known for years the power of events to distract us
from bouts of wearying numbness. You see,
I grew up with hurricanes, or their threat. Wind,
waves, crashing coconuts. Twenty years

before my birth, a famous storm
washed a chest of sterling flatware onto a lawn
along Bayshore Drive. Little wonder

I hired on at newspapers, reporting
on rapes, murders, fires, bored only in the lulls
between. You can guess where I'm heading,
Mrs. C. Is it fair to speculate
that Eliacim's death erased the need
for you to distract yourself with anything but grief?

I confess that for most of my life
I've let events keep me from turning
the compost of my soul. Worse, I've allowed my son—
his own accidents and derailments—to churn
my life into the kind of sea that washes up no silver.

Loss Considers the Idea of Bliss

He's not exactly opposed to it,
as he would be opposed to grime, say,
or certain kinds of odors. It's more a matter
of weight, he supposes, or timing. Something less
sublime, less fleshy, would suit him better.
He thinks of the windy give in every given,
the corpulent hope now decomposing,
John Hinckley's mom, before switching on the TV,
happy at her ironing.

You Can't Write Off the Dead

A friend wrote me off once, as did a cousin,
and I was as good as dead to them
but infinitely better
because I kept my distance.
The dead don't.
They're invasive, like those scilla I'm still digging out
of my garden, wheeling the clumps
across the street onto city property, where they'll bloom
their blue heads off long after I'm gone.
The dead won't go
across the street. They hate city property.
True, you no longer have to trim their thick toenails
or yank the stiff hair that grows straight out
of the chin. But you remember
how you lofted the tweezers to the brazen light,
triumphant,
while the stunned air radiated pain.

To Lose Something

A Philip Larkin poem, for instance, which you tore
from *The New Yorker,* though, of course,

you can't remember the title, only that you loved it
and you know if you found it you could finally begin

your morning. Or that black and white photo
of the gaggle of preschoolers in the town

where your grandparents lived, the town
you only visited but the teachers treated you

as one of their own. Find that, and you're home.
You remember how the camera caught the class

squinting into morning sun and how the plump girl
in back was hiking her skirt to scratch

her leg. What eludes you is what you wore,
and whether your cousin with the bowl

of yellow hair stood to your left or right.
It may take hours to locate them, Larkin's poem

evaporating by the second, the photo fading.
But wait. Larkin was talking about

whether what's over is past, or if one season
simply allows a path into the next. So you ask,

all these decades later: Are we children lined up
that May morning gone, sun no longer bathing

our faces? Or are we merely in transit,
the grass beneath our feet mown

and mown again, as we begin and begin,
new and the same, for the rest of our days?

III

The Dual Nature
of Grief

Briefly, I Was Asleep

on the sofa—quick nap—
hand curled
under my chin, my mother curled
in me. Explain, you say.
It's as if she came swimming
up my limbs, so that
briefly
I felt as I did as a girl
helping her in the kitchen—
when I would stir the sauce,
my bent elbow
seemed to become
her bent elbow,
my hand
fastened to the circling spoon,
her hand,
so that she inhabited me,
knuckle and wrist,
length and bend,
a presence
more emphatic than my own.

The Stepping-Stone Kit

If only, my dear, I had one of your hands cast in plaster and cut off at the wrist.

—Mrs. Caldwell

Last spring, Mrs. C., when my son visited—
not a successful visit, I might add—
I bought a stepping-stone kit, complete
with cement mix and directions. We gathered
the sea shells he'd brought for his daughter,
and the two pressed their hands into the wet
concrete. Around their prints, we embedded the shells,
giving the whole the look of a cheap gift
bought in haste at a beach resort.

Do I mind? Mrs. Caldwell, surely you know
better. I placed this treasure in my shade garden,
near the trunk of the *Viburnam carlesi,* close
to the ferns. By midsummer,
my granddaughter began to worry
the stone had been stolen. I knew it was
there, of course, but we launched a vigorous search
and found it, cool and damp, under the fronds.

Mrs. C., I sincerely wish you'd had a stepping-stone kit
when Eliacim was alive. No, it's not the same
as a son who calls out in his beloved voice, *Hello!*
Anybody home? But I must say, it's dearer
to me than hundreds of his photographs.
Each day, I can bend and press my hand into his.

48

I Took My Mother Shopping

after she died.
So much easier this way.
She could walk again,
and she liked orange
chiffon and skirts
that flared.
She was looser
with the clerks, joking,
smiling. We were like girls again,
twirling around
the dressing room,
whistling at ourselves
in the mirror. I was so glad
to have my mother back.
I hoped she'd never take off
that sparkly black sheath
she was trying now, wiggling
her hips. I thought of questions
I'd been wanting to ask,
stories I'd saved up.
All so amiable, so amicable,
the colors, the fabrics,
the fitting room
with its flocked chairs
and thick carpet. All those
glad, gossamer things.

I Knew a Boy

whose mother would bundle him up
before bed, drive bar to bar, shooing him
inside to look for his dad. Heading home,
they'd stop at the tracks,
the boy's flashlight scouring the rails.

We've all gripped something, trying
to find those we lose
too soon. My favorite cousin
to suicide—*Love Is Eternal,* he wrote
on a scrap—and one of my sons to drink.

Years ago, I put away
my flashlight. Drag them home, they go back
out. Next time, night hangs heavier
in the alleys, the streets blow
colder. When he calls, I listen.
When he doesn't, I remember when
he was three, how he loved to lap
from the dog's yellow bowl, his tongue
working like mad.

The Best I Can Do For Her

My mother died a couple of years ago. I wasn't there to see it . . .
But these are the shrouds to wrap her in. They're . . . the best
I can do for her.

—Lucas Samara, an exhibit of his quilts, Athens, Greece

I wasn't there either when my mother died,
alone, on her side, the way she swam,
the way for years I made fun of, until I found myself
last Sunday swimming on my own side
in an aquamarine ocean far from home.
She would've loved the Aegean, its breezes
streaked with salt and lemon.

At water's edge, I gathered green stones,
filling my sunhat with the glistening
pebbles, sorting by hue. Too soft, a jeweler told me,
for rings or bracelets. But beautiful, she agreed.
I crammed dozens into my suitcase, no idea how
I would use them.

I dreamed last night that suitcase was stolen, snatched
from my side as I waited for a glass elevator
to deliver me to my mother's old room, No. 275,
which I can still smell, its blend of lavender
and decay. Instead, I was hurled
into space and floated in air so vast I saw nothing
for miles. I woke before I landed,
but I know I had my hands out—dying
to surprise her with green.

51

Why I Miss Visiting My Mother-in-Law in Helena, Arkansas

From way out there,
everything at home seemed enchanted,
our yellow bungalow
under the willow oaks,
that swaybacked block
of cheese in the fridge, damp
with longing. Our tub with its shoreline
of ragged caulking, grown suddenly
sleek. My lingerie relaxing
in its drawer, silkier, more secret.
Our down pillows, their glad floating.

And the fairy tale air
of the living room, its hint
of cool near the hearth.
The dining room, our best plates
laid out, those white lakes of anticipation.

Our books
reading themselves
to sleep, muffling their sobs.
The faded blue towels itching
for the slope of our shoulders.

My mother-in-law died,
and I miss her—she made
a tasty remoulade
and sensational Millionaire Pie.

But mostly, I miss visiting her
in Helena, Arkansas, because now
our house is only
what it is—imperfect and unglazed.

The Villa

She thought we lived there, in that painting
beside her bed. A villa
on the Mediterranean, a path to the sea,
wisteria playing off
the sun-buffed walls. *That's you
climbing the hill,* my mother would say
in the weeks before she died. *Look.
Loaves of bread in your arms.*

That painting now hangs
in my house, and I've come to believe
we do inhabit the place. You cannot see
inside, but I know
there's a dining room with a bank
of flung windows where I am five
again and she is teaching me to set a table

I can barely reach: fork on the left,
cutting edge of knife turned
toward the plate. I must use all my wits
to do this, as she drifts in
and out, hands lighting here, here,
nails polished red
as on the day she died, breezes blowing white
across the years, a row of lemons on the sill.

I Want to Write a Poem I'd Be Too Embarrassed to Read to My Monday Night Poetry Group

a poem demanding
and insistent, like a letter
I'd stashed away, now exposed,
confessing to something obscene—
like those mannequins I keep
crammed in my attic, the ones I dress
and re-dress to resemble my late mother,
their silver wigs and clip-on earrings,
the pocketbooks and gloves
from the fifties, their bosoms, deep
and fragrant, their faces radiant,
and all those flesh-toned arms
outstretched, waiting to enfold me.

The Dual Nature of Grief

*Do you know, Eliacim, the feelings of wood, the love, the responsibility,
the fear, the hatred, the loyalty, the purity of wood?*

—Mrs. Caldwell

You write to your son, who's decomposing
in the Aegean, that to sleep in a bed
of pure wood is not the same
as sleeping in a bed
of irresponsible wood. On and on you go.

How silly, Mrs. C. You know as well as I
that no wood is completely pure
nor entirely irresponsible.
In most varieties, light and dark mingle,
lending a capricious cast to the whole.

So it is with grief. It will drag us
deep and excite us
to ecstasy.
Understand, please, Mrs. C., I envy
your excesses, your *grande jetés*
of the spirit. But let us admit
our wicked secret. You could not rise
to such a pitch—dare I say it?—had Eliacim lived.

Loss Hungers for Something

A path through the woods,
an elusive scent, a glimpse of cattails, lakeside
turbulence. The notion is vague, slow
to take a shape. Children playing, lawns shifting
in shade, green seeping to green,
that old leafy discontent.

A Place Airy and Fraught

with a high-pitched wind. No trees
or flowers. Only a pale circle of grass
and bowers of emptiness.

Not a place you'd invite friends,
as to a mountain retreat. I had a choice.
At least that's how it seems now.

Two shakes and I'd have been back
at my door, Lady Banks roses spilling
behind the hedge

of miniature box. Did I mention the twist
to the wind in this place, how it trips me
into a kind of giddiness,

a state I'd have sworn to you I deplore
were it not for this barefoot frenzy,
this crazed thirsting for more.